The Tao of Loss and Grief

The Tao of Loss and Grief

Lao Tzu's Tao Te Ching Adapted for New Emotions

Pamela Metz

Humanics Trade Group
Atlanta - Frankfurt - Paris

The Tao of Loss and Grief
A Humanics Trade Group Publication

Brumby Holdings, LLC
1197 Peachtree Street
Suite 533 Plaza
Atlanta, GA 30361

Printed in the United States of America

ISBN: 0-89334-335-8

Publisher Dedication

Melissa Jayne

Table of Contents

Acknowledgments

I thank all of the people who have been supportive and helpful on my path. I am especially grateful to those people who have read earlier drafts of this and other works, students who have caused me to know in unspoken ways, and my friends, family and colleagues who are always there. The patients, families and coworkers at the Hospice of Peace were my teachers for this book and I remember them with every word in it. I am pleased to work with Gary Wilson and the Humanics Publishing Group as they continue the tradition of bringing adaptations of Lao Tzu's Tao Te Ching to readers around the world.

Introduction

The Tao of Loss and Grief provides the reader with a gentle philosophy of life and living based upon Lao Tzu's classic Tao te Ching. The Tao (literally, "the way") of grieving acknowledges the mysteries of life and its many difficulties and surprises. Loss and the responding emotional response of grief are part of the mysterious whole of life. In this experience are also hope, love, forgiveness, and recovery from the loss.

The book is written to be read from beginning to end and/or to be read by selecting chapters from the Table of Contents. Opening it at random is another way to trust in the gentle words of guidance so helpful in the journeys of loss and grief. Reading the book at various times during the grieving process may help the reader see some progress through the experiences of grieving.

1. No One Way

The Tao of loss and grief
takes many forms.

There is no one way
to walk through life's sorrows.

In this mystery
is found the beginnings
of all things.

Caught up in the difficulties
you cannot see any hope.

Yet, there are many possibilities
for traveling this path.

Though darkness persists,
there is the light of understanding
that there is no one way.

2. Finding Your Way

When your life seems difficult
other lives may seem easy.
When other people are happy
your way is sad.

Opposites are part of the one-ness.
These opposites create each other:

Tears and smiles are human emotions
Giving and receiving are natural cycles
Work and rest are necessary companions.

So, if you can
weep without tears,
speak without words,
watch without grasping,
understand without possessing,
listen to the silence,

you will find your own way
to do the work of grieving.

3. Grief Work

If you think other people
have found the way
You may not be present
to find your own.

Can you begin
by opening your mind and heart
to make room for the work of grief?

When confusion enters,
can you wait with it?

If you can make a place
and a time for grieving,
your grief work has begun.

4. Infinite Tao

The Tao of loss and grief is infinite:
It is experienced,
but never completed.
It is filled with life.

You cannot see it,
but it is always with you.
It is as constant as
the sun and stars.

5. Supports for the Journey

Loss does not take sides;
It happens to good and bad alike.
The Tao does not take sides;
It welcomes all the people in the world.

The Tao of grieving is like
the springtime.
It is beautiful, yet it
comes of winter.

It is a part of
the seasons of life.
The more you embrace
the cycles of nature,
the more your work
can be integrated.

Keep fast to your path.

6. Strengths

The Tao is like Mother Nature:
Invisible and yet evident
in the birth of all things.

The strength of the Tao is within you.
You can call upon it at any time.

7. Letting Go

The Tao is forever.
Why is this?

The Tao is available
to all of us
because it desires nothing
for itself.

If you can wait
then you will go ahead.
If you can let go
you will not be left alone.
If you can become lost
in your grief,
You will find your own way through.

8. Your Own Way

Your own way is like the water:
it is necessary to all living things.
Your way is like the Tao,
it seeks the places that feel
low and empty.

In your daily living, remain centered.
In your thinking, remain hopeful.
In your feelings, embrace sorrow.
In work, be gentle with yourself.
In family, with friends, attempt to be present.

When you are willing to go your own way
through loss and grief;

When you do not compare yourself
with the ways of others,

You will be a guide for those
who follow.

9. A Way to Peace

Try to deny your grief
and it will grow stronger.

Avoid the pain of loss
and it becomes worse.

Pretend that you are okay
and the truth will be heard.

Protect others from knowing
and they wonder what is wrong.

Do your work in grieving and then let go.
This is the only way to peace.

10. Getting Through

Are you able to stay focused
on the importance of your loss?
Are you able to stay flexible to
the ups and downs of this path?
Are you able to clear your eyes
in order to see the light?
Are you able to love the people in your life
while you experience your grief?
Are you able to work at the demands of daily life
while feeling the pain of grief?
Are you able to see your loss
in the larger picture of life?

Give yourself credit for the ways
you are getting through your grief.

11. Emptiness Within

Our bodies are whole,
but there is emptiness within.

We move and speak,
but it is without life.

We sleep and eat,
but we wonder why.

We are empty within,
but full of sorrow.

12. Inner Views

The lights are too bright.

The noise is deafening.

Food has no taste.

The mind cannot think.

The heart is heavy with loss.

Observe the world,
but trust your inner view.
Let these things come and go
and be as open as the night sky.

13. Faith

Numbness is not better than feelings.
Denial is as difficult as reality.

Why is numbness not better than feelings?
If you do not feel anything,
you are missing life.
Either way, your faith is at risk.

Why is denial as difficult as reality?
Both denial and reality are
forms of existence.
Which existence do you choose?

Keep your faith in the way things are.
If you can live in the world,
and accept loss and grief,
then you can love again.

14. Origins

When you look, you can't see it.
When you listen, you can't hear it.
When you grasp it, it slips away.

When there is no darkness,
When there is no light,
When there is no form, no image, no nothing...

Find that there is no beginning.
Realize that there is no end.
Understand that there is no knowing.

When you discover your origins,
this is the beginning of healing.

15. Waiting

The people who came before us down this path
gave us ways to understand.

They survived, even though
they did not know the way.
They remained, even though
their losses were great.
They continued, even though
they did not know how.
They gave us hope,
even though they had none
at the time.

Can you wait
until this pain passes
and your vision becomes clear?
Can you remain still
until the next steps emerge?

Waiting gives you permission
to be open to the possibilities.

16. Gifts from the Universe

Open your heart to the universe.
Let your mind be clear and free.
Acknowledge the problems and difficulties.
And welcome the solutions and resolutions.

Every living being in the world
returns home at last.
Coming home is a gift
from the universe
that gave us life.

If we do not recognize the gifts,
we become confused and sad.
If we remember how
we came to be,
we are free to be
gentle, loving, accepting
and strong.

In this awe of the universe,
we can cope with these times.

When it is time to return,
we are ready.

17. Help from Others

When our world is whole,
we take it for granted.

When loss occurs,
we seek out
help from others.

It is important to trust
the people who
reach out to us.

Those who help us
the most,
are those who help us see
that we are able
to help ourselves!

18. In Loss, Gain?

How can there be gain
in the middle of loss?

When darkness fades
then light appears.

After rain, comes the sun.

When healing helps,
we receive our gifts.

When winter dies,
spring is born.

19. The Way Things Are

Let go of preconceptions,
and you see what is.

Let go of sorrow and anger,
and feel the softness in your heart.

Let go of letting go,
and realize how much you have.

If you cannot do these things,
be still and listen to the universe.

Become aware of the way things are.

20. Unique Paths

If you stop grieving,
will your problems end?
What is the difference
between loss and healing?
Can another's path show you
the way to your own?

When others grieve,
they must do so
in their own ways.

When you grieve,
it is important
to follow
your own unique journey
on this path.

21. At One with Oneself

If you are able
to be at one with the Tao
then you are able
to be at one with yourself.

But, the Tao cannot be held.
How can one be with it?
Because you give in to it.

But, the Tao is elusive and mysterious.
How can one hold it dear?
Because you let it be dear.

Because the Tao is,
it surpasses time and place.
How can we understand this?
Because we remain
at one with ourselves.

22. Becoming Whole Again

To become whole again,
let yourself fall apart.

To heal the pain,
let yourself feel the pain.

To feel at peace,
let yourself be in conflict.

To renew your faith,
let yourself be unfaithful.

To return to living,
let yourself be lost.

Those who have survived grief
give us hope for the path ahead.
Because they are silent,
we listen for their words.
Because they trust the process,
we trust in our own process.

When you give in to the experiences of loss,
you can become whole again.

23. Giving Voice to Grief

Give your grief sound,
then remain silent.
Be close to nature:
When it storms, there is noise and confusion.
When it is hot, there is the sun.
When the storms abate, there is relief and calm.

When you are open to the Tao,
you become one with the Tao
and you can be full of understanding.
When you are open to grief,
you become one with grief
and you can give it its natural voice.
When you are open to loss,
you become one with loss
and you can begin the healing of acceptance.

Stay open to the Tao,
and trust your natural instincts;
everything in life has its place.

24. Letting Go Again

When you become unbalanced
you feel out of sorts.
When you rush the process
you don't go fast.
When you pretend you're fine
you deny your pain.
When you avoid others
you miss their support and caring.
When you cling to your loss
you have no room for new gifts.

If you seek comfort from the Tao,
grieve your loss, then let go again.

25. The Tao Before the Universe

Before the universe came to be,
there was something without form.
It is calm. Spacious.
Mysterious. Immutable.
Without borders. Always present.
It gave birth to the universe
and is called the Tao.

It is present in everything,
before and after,
without and within.
It returns to the beginnings
of every thing.

The Tao is powerful.
The universe is powerful.
The planet is powerful.
Human beings are powerful.
These are powerful energies.

Humans are of the earth.
Earth is of the universe.
The universe is of the Tao.
The Tao is of itself.

26. Staying in Touch with Yourself

Opposites give us
some understanding of life.
Light and dark.
Stillness and motion.

Therefore, you may travel in your mind
without leaving your home.
Regardless of the temptations,
it is important to stay in touch with yourself.

Why should you accept invitations
and abandon your place of comfort?
If you allow yourself to
go hither and yon,
you may lose touch with your soul.
If you allow the world to move you,
you may interrupt your own grief process.

27. The Journey of Loss

The journey of loss has no destination.
Travelers may not know when they have arrived.

The journey of loss is guided
by time and the unknown.

The journey of loss takes
the traveler with an open mind.

The Tao of grief is possible for all people
and no one is turned away.
All situations can be helpful,
and the path becomes clear.

When people grieve badly,
they show us that way to grieve.

When people understand
that loss is a journey,
they are on their way
to peace.

28. Ups and Downs

When you are feeling down
remember that there is also up.
Remain open to the world
and the Tao will be with you.
You are a beginner.

Remember the day,
even in the darkness of night.
This is how the world is.
The Tao remains with you
throughout it all.

Your loss is personal,
others do not feel it.
Accept this as part of the world.
The Tao is part of the world
and holds you through the difficulties.

The world came from nothing,
like mushrooms after the rain.
Remember that you are
a part of all things.

29. A Time for All Things

Do you wonder when the pain
of loss will soften?

Grieving is a sacred journey.
It cannot be rushed.
If you deny it, it will persist.
If you send it away, it will return.

There is a time for all things,
a time for feeling sad,
a time for feeling happy;
a time for being restless,
a time for being still;
a time for being exhausted,
a time for being energized;
a time for wandering,
a time for being at home.

If you can see things as they unfold
without trying to manage them;
If you can let your grief go its own way,
you will return to the center of your life.

30. Waiting in the Void

If you are able to trust in the Tao
and don't try to force your process,
you remain in the protection of this way.
Forcing, even with good intentions,
comes back to the sender.

If you can grieve your loss
and then wait,
you can understand that
the world is not in our control.
Trying to force the process
goes against the flow of the Tao.
If you can believe in yourself,
you do not have to confront others.
If you can wait in the void,
you can find your way to the sun.
Because you can accept your own way,
others accept you as well.

31. Sorrow and Compassion

Avoidance can create difficulties;
people may choose this path.

Sorrow and compassion
can support people through their grief.

Healing is the highest value
and remains as constant possibility.

If others don't understand
it is better to forgive them.
How could we not forgive their fears?

Stay on your journey
with gentle resolve,
giving to others
that which you desire yourself.

32. Comfort in the Tao

You can't see the Tao.
It is both large and small.

If people could find comfort
in the Tao,
we would be in balance.
People would find peace
and their hearts would be full.

Know that this time of grieving
is temporary.
Know that there is purpose
in this part of life.
Knowing this,
you may find comfort.

The Tao comforts all things
as mothers care for their young.

33. Embracing Loss

Knowing yourself
is part of the process of grief.
Embracing your loss
allows it to be free.

When you understand
that life is a gift,
then loss becomes
a part of life.

If you can stand firm
and embrace your loss,
then you are full
of the knowledge of life.

34. Lost in the Tao

The spirit of the Tao
is everywhere.
Everything is part of it,
yet the Tao does not
create everything.
It is part of all things
but does not own them.

Because the Tao
makes no claims,
it creates its own
special spirit.

35. Finding Peace

When you are centered
in the Tao
you may find peace
even in the midst of sorrow.

Life continues to present
challenges and uncertainty.
The Tao may seem elusive
and without meaning.
When your eyes seek it,
it is hidden.
When your ears listen,
it is silent.
When you trust in it,
you may find peace.

36. Hurt and Healing

If you want to heal,
you must first allow yourself to feel the pain.
If you want to recover,
you must first acknowledge the difficulty.
If you want to be rid of something,
you must first admit that you have it.
This is sometimes known as the way things are.

Healing overcomes the hurt.
Time moves at different speeds.
Allow your process to be mysterious.
Trust that you are on your way.

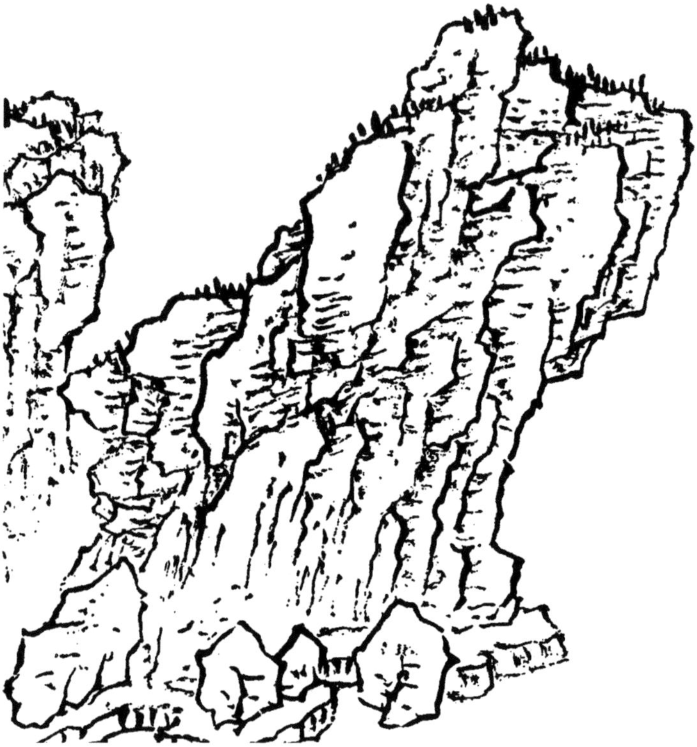

37. Trust in the Tao

The Tao can be trusted
because it is part of the whole.

If you can imagine yourself
in the Tao,
it is possible to be transformed
by following a natural path.

Can you be content
with the daily unfolding of life?
Can you trust in the world
and free yourself of uncertainty?

When you trust in the Tao
you create peace in your world.

38. Behind the Loss

Can you use the power you have
to understand the loss?
In understanding the loss,
can you see the unfinished business?

Even people who understand
remain incomplete in their understanding.
Those who rush about
leave much that is not done.

Kind people work hard,
yet leave some things unfinished.
Able people do many things,
yet many things are left undone.
Caring people reach out,
and when we cannot respond,
they continue to care.

In the midst of chaos,
seek behind the loss.
Concern yourself with reality
and know that you are in the Tao.

39. Part of the Whole

When our world is whole
our hearts are light and full.
Content with our lives
we give no thought to loss.

When loss occurs,
our outlook changes,
our hearts are heavy,
our awareness changes the world.

Can you view yourself with compassion
because you are part of the whole?
Can you be formed by the Tao,
smoothed and made a part of the whole?

40. Birth Rites

The Tao moves in ways mysterious.
Accepting is the way of the Tao.

You were born into the world,
coming from the mystery of the universe.
Accepting loss as a rite of birth,
you understand the way of life.

41. Contradictions

When some people hear about the Tao,
they embrace it immediately.
When other people hear of the Tao,
they question its existence.
When a few people hear of the Tao,
they ridicule it.
If they didn't, it wouldn't be the Tao.

The path of grieving is filled with contradictions:
When going toward the light, the path becomes dark.
When going forward, the path goes backwards.
When pain is unbearable, there is some relief.
When weakness prevails, strength returns.
When vision is blurred, the view becomes clear.
When love is lost, understanding is found.

The Tao cannot be found,
yet it provides unity in the contradictions of all things.

42. Being Alone

When loss occurs
we become aware
of being alone.
Loss gives birth to all things.

A woman is part of a man.
A man is part of a woman.
Males and females
are part of the balance of all things.

When feeling alone,
can you embrace your solitude,
feeling your oneness with the world?

43. Gentle Learning

Softness overcomes the hard.
That which is gentle
flows past the obstacles of tears.
Trust in the learning that is happening.

Learning without words,
teaching without doing.
This is the way of the Tao.

44. Grieve in Your Own Way

How important is it to you to be healed?

Which is more valuable to you, sadness or rest?

Which is more difficult, succeeding or failing?

If you depend on others for your healing,
you may lose your own way.
If you believe that you will never be happy,
you create unhappiness within yourself.

Grieve in your own way:
Accept the way things are.
When you begin to realize how to go forward,
you understand the meaning of the loss to you.

45. Allowing the Hurt to Happen

Healing seems impossible,
yet healing does happen.
Hurting seems to be reality,
yet other things matter also.

Everything seems difficult.
Thinking is slow.
Fog covers all.

By allowing the hurt to happen,
you begin to heal the wounds.
If you can stay on the path,
the Tao heals you to wholeness.

46. Fear and Anger

When you are grieving a loss,
fear and anger can be felt.
When you become stuck in your grief work,
everything in life seems stuck also.

It is natural to feel fear and anger
in the face of change,
in the emptiness of loss.

If you can live through fear and anger,
you will find your way to safety.

47. Doing Nothing

By staying in one place,
you can be in touch with the world.
By being at home,
you can sense the presence of the Tao.

The more you seek,
the less you find.

Can you be here without leaving,
see the truth without looking,
do grief work by doing nothing?

48. Less and Less

We are taught
that we should
accumulate things.
The Tao teaches
that less is more.

When you understand not to force things,
you eventually reach a place of doing nothing.
When you do less,
everything gets done.

True healing happens
by allowing the work to go its own way.
Interfering with this way may obstruct the process.

49. Other People

By keeping an open mind
you can be present to other people.

If you can be present
to both good and bad people,
you experience true goodness.

If you can trust in people who are helpful
and those who are not,
you experience the trust.

If you feel that
other people don't understand you,
take your time.
Eventually, you will find your way.

50. Surrendering

Can you surrender to your loss
and to whatever the day may bring?

All things are lost eventually
and we are left with nothing.
Our minds and bodies
understand that this is so.

If you let your life
come from the center of your soul;
If you hold nothing back
and surrender to the truth;

Then you are ready for life
in the way that the sun rises
at the beginning of a new day.

51. Part of the Tao, Part of Nature

Everything is part of the Tao.
All of us take life
from the source of the Tao.
This is why we are a part of nature.

Because we all come
from the Tao,
we are born,
nurtured, comforted,
protected.

We all return someday
to the Tao,
just as everything in nature
returns to the source.

52. Opening Your Heart

The Tao was in the beginning.
Everything comes from it;
everything returns to it.

To find the beginning,
remember where you came from.
When you remember,
you will begin to heal
from your loss.

If you open your heart
you create the way for peace.
If you close your heart,
you will continue in your sorrow.

When you can see through the darkness,
you will find light.
Use your light to find the source.
Opening your heart,
you are on the journey.

53. Not in the Tao

The path of healing
is open to you.
When you can't find it,
stay with the spirit of the Tao.

When your heart hurts
while others are free;
When darkness prevails
even in the brightness of day;
When emptiness persists
even in the fullness of life;

Then you know that
you are not in the Tao.
Stay centered
and trust in the Tao.

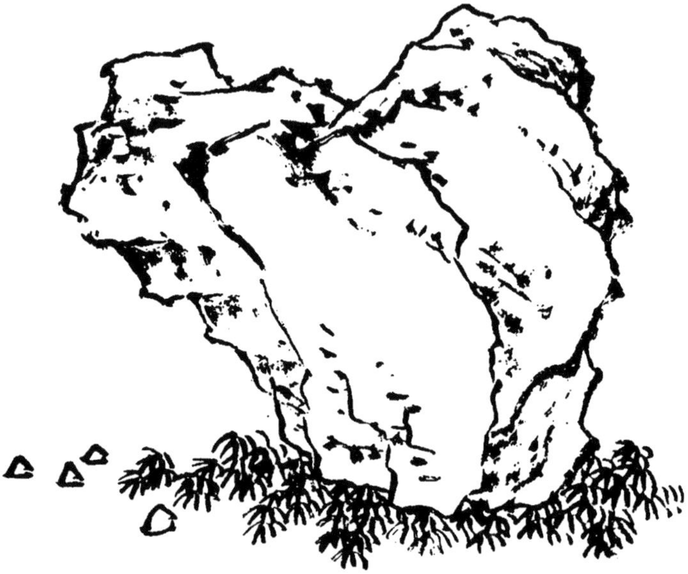

54. Tao in Your Life

When you stay centered
in the Tao,
you cannot be moved.
When you hold the Tao close,
it will not go away.
You can remember this feeling
from moment to moment.

If you allow the Tao
to be present in your living,
you will begin to see its truths.

If you allow the Tao
to be present in your family,
they will respond to this spirit.

If you allow the Tao
to be present in your community,
your community will grow and prosper.

If you allow the Tao
to be present in your world,
your world will welcome the Tao.

You can find this truth
when you look inside yourself.

55. Beginning Again

After a loss, it is necessary to begin again.
Like a baby, we must learn about our new world.
Like a baby, we cry until comforted,
we seek harmony with our environment,
and sleep when we are tired.
In beginning again we find harmony
in our lives.

Can you let yourself
let go so the new can find you?
Can you let go of expectations
so your disappointments fade?
Can you let your spirit renew
so you are able to begin again?

56. Resting

When you don't know, keep silent.
When you need rest, keep still.

Take time out,
stop moving.
Close your eyes.
Slow your breathing.
Let the telephone ring.
Doing this allows you to be resting.

Like the Tao,
you can not be interrupted,
disturbed or distracted,
pitied or pursued.
If you take the rest when you need it,
you will endure this time.

57. Knowing When to Stop

If you are on the journey of grief,
you must know when to stop.
If you let go of expectations and outcomes,
the journey will find its own end.

When others expect you to be grieving,
your grief will find no end.
When you look at a calendar,
the days seem endless and difficult.
When you fear the worst,
the worst may find you eventually.

Therefore, consider the possibilities:
I let go of my loss
and the loss is less painful.
I let go of my pain
and my pain is transformed.
I let go of my fears
and peace returns to my heart.
I let go of the finite
and life becomes infinite.

58. Friends and Family

When friends and family
stand firmly by;
When neighbors and co-workers
allow you to grieve;
The world becomes a place
to live the loss to recovery.

If people push too hard,
the process becomes too hard.
If family members resist,
the process becomes resistance.
If friends choose not to call,
the process becomes undone.

Can you allow yourself
to be an example
of how this process unfolds?
You give a gift to others
simply by being yourself.

59. Balance

When grieving a loss
it is important to find balance.

The ability to stretch
keeps a person supple.
Opening to what happens,
you let life in, like sunlight
after the night.
If you can see that there is no ending
then everything is part of the whole.

When you seek balance,
everything is possible.
When you let go,
balance is in the nature of things.

60. Grief Works

Grief works because
it is a part of life.
It does not need
too much interference.

Stay in the center
of the Tao
and the work
will begin to get done.

We grieve
that which we love.
Sadness is
the other side of joy.
Give yourself time
to experience the whole process.

61. Rivers of Tears

When a loss occurs,
it becomes the center of living.
Tears flow like rivers
into a sea of uncertainty.
The larger the loss,
the greater the sea of sadness.

Living through the loss
requires great strengths:
One is recognizing the loss.
Two is accepting the pain of the loss.
Three is grieving the loss.
Four is adjusting to life without the lost object.
Five is investing energy into something new.

If you can do these things
you will be living in the Tao.
You will find that tears
can water the seeds of tomorrow.

62. Beyond Price

In the center of the universe is the Tao.
It can be a gift
and a place of rest.

Things can be bought with money;
respect comes from doing good things;
because the Tao is beyond price,
no one can buy it.

Can you be helpful
when being with others?
Can you understand
and teach about the Tao?

Why is the Tao respected?
When you are in the Tao,
you find what you seek.
When you are mistaken,
you are forgiven.
This is why the Tao is respected.

63. Going Through it, Not Over It

Go through your grief,
not over it.
Take each small step
to create the larger ones.
Face each difficulty
in the beginning
and the way will be less difficult.
Walk through your grief
by taking a number of small steps.

If you don't try to go over it,
you will find your way through it.
When you bump into obstacles,
stop and wait with your feelings.
Be not afraid for your safety,
you are already safe in the Tao.

64. Planning Ahead

What you plant is easy to nurture.
What is new is easy to change.
What is fragile is easy to shatter,
What is tiny is easy to disperse.

Prevent difficulties by planning ahead.
Put things in their places as you find them.
Rivers grow from a single drop of water.
Going through grief begins
with a series of small steps.

Putting the loss out of your mind, you remember.
Trying to hold on, your grip slips.
Forcing grief to be over,
the journey never ends.

Can you allow your journey
to take its own course?
Can you find the calm
that follows the storm?
Do you remember how
to let go of what you don't have?
If you can care for the Tao,
you can care for all things.
Planning ahead
takes you into the future.

65. Watching Others

Other people may grieve
in their own ways.
Some will weep;
Others remain silent.

When you watch others,
remember that is their way.
Stay centered in the Tao
to find your own way.

As you learn how to grieve,
you may need to unlearn
the ways of others.
The most natural ways
are the ways to follow.
Have faith that there
is rest after a long journey.

66. No Comparisons

Staying receptive keeps us humble.
Not comparing gives us freedom.

By not comparing our process,
we are free to find our own ways.
Meeting others' expectations,
we lose sight of our own.

The sun shines on everyone
and no one is better than another.
The stars remain
and each one deserves its home.
The world receives their lights
because we do not compare their processes.

67. Feeling the Pain of Loss

It could be said that
this teaching makes no sense.
Some might think it interesting
but obscure.
If you can reflect upon these words,
you may find comfort and understanding.

The most difficult lessons
are to feel the pain of loss:
Accept that the loss has happened.
Allow yourself to feel the pain.
Adjust to the changes from the loss.
Invest yourself in new relationships.

Being patient in these processes
and compassionate with yourself,
you begin to recover from the effects
of the loss in your life.

68. Harmony and Living

Because we like others
to be their best,
we seek the best
in ourselves.

Harmony in living
comes from not competing with others.
Live in the spirit of playfulness,
like a child running on grass.
When you can be as a child,
you are living in harmony with the Tao.

69. Wait and See

There is a saying:
"Instead of making the first move
it is better to wait and see.
Instead of going forward a step
it may be better to step back."

This can be thought of
as moving forward without improvement,
fighting back without using words.

Difficulty is great
when grief is not understood.
Lack of understanding
keeps you in the dark.
This can destroy your spirit
and you may harm yourself.

When you meet your grief,
understand the process:
stepping back may move you ahead.

70. Who Are You Now?

When a loss happens
we are no longer the same person.
It is hard to remember
that we must define ourselves yet again.

How can we understand
that we must ask the question
who am I now?

71. Mysteries of Healing

Not knowing how to heal
is the beginning of healing.
When you realize you are grieving
then you have begun the process.

You are your own healer.
If you embrace the mysteries,
you become whole again.

72. Spirituality and Religion

When people find themselves in the dark,
they seek a source of light.
When all they've known is taken from them,
they look for new ways of knowing.

Can you trust in the teachings
that have come before?
Can you accept that
there is really nothing forgotten?

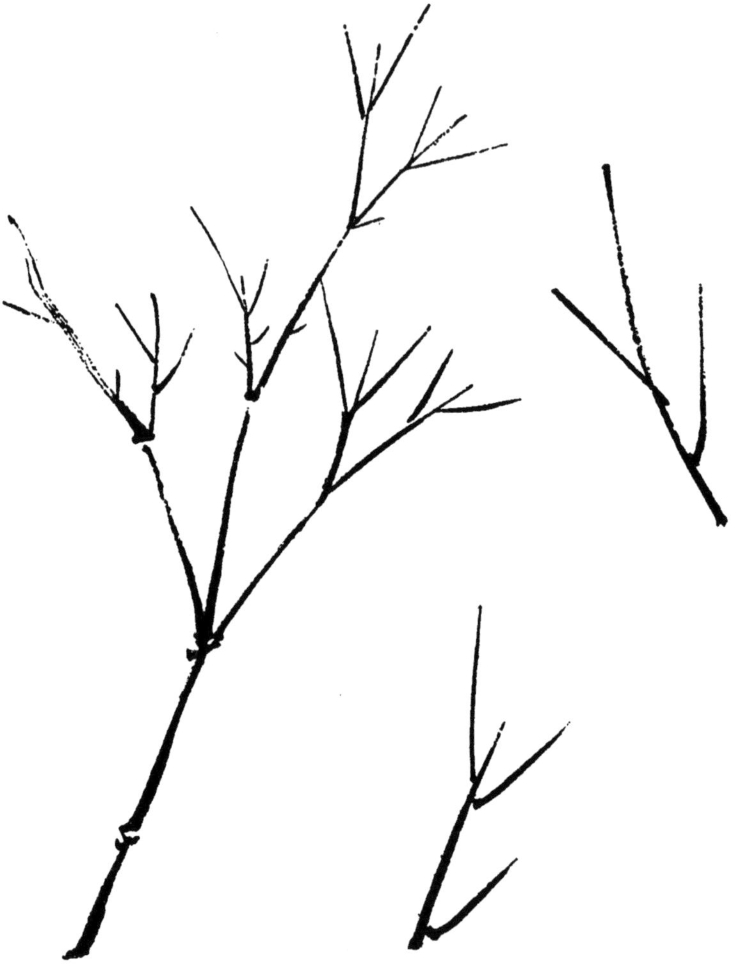

73. Tao is Always Present

The Tao is always present.
It exists without our awareness.
It comforts without form
answers in silence
surrounds us in our solitude.

It is everywhere in the world.
Without being seen,
it sees all without fail.

74. Beyond Our Understanding

When we realize that everything changes,
then we cannot hold on to any thing.
When we are not afraid of loss,
then anything is possible.

When we realize that
much is beyond our understanding,
we are free from trying to control.
When we try to control,
we are likely to fail.

75. Resources

When we require too much,
there is less for others.
When people interfere,
it is difficult to progress.

Use the resources that are available.
Ask for what you need.
Trust your own process.

76. Yielding to Life

In our beginnings we are soft and flexible;
in our endings we become dry and brittle.
Nature teaches us to yield
so we may pass through
the narrow places of life.

Can you be like the willow
and bend in the winds of your life?
Can you yield like water
to flow around obstacles in your path?

Staying rigid and tense makes you vulnerable.
Being soft and flexible
will lead you through this passage of life.

77. Giving and Grieving

When grieving in the Tao
you can be flexible:
Some days are solitary
and alone.
Other days you can be
open and give to others.
Staying balanced
is never easy.

When we try to control
our daily ups and downs,
we go against the nature of the Tao.
We give to those who already have
and take away from those in need.

Can you keep giving
even when grieving?
Can you be present
even with a broken heart?
Can you accept
that life follows loss?

78. In the Middle of Sorrow

Can you rest in your sorrow
as water in a quiet pond?
Can you be patient
as ice melting in spring?

The gentle outlasts the firm;
the yielding overcomes resistance.
We may understand these truths,
but it is difficult to practice them.

Can you then remain
in the middle of your sorrow?
Because you stay centered
others cannot harm you.

This understanding will
lead you through your sorrow.

79. No Mistakes

When you feel you are mistaken
it is an opportunity to try again.

When you understand
your journey,
you can find the path.
You can do what is needed
and not worry about mistakes.

80. Going On

If a life is to be lived wisely
a person will find contentment.
People can enjoy the gifts
from the universe
and forget what they don't possess.
Because people value their existence
they need not travel far.
There may be planes and cars,
but these are not on the person's path.
There may be telephones and computers
but these are diversions from the path.

You may enjoy eating,
spending time with friends and family,
taking walks and planting a garden,
enjoying the life in the community.
Even though distractions are always available
with promises of forgetfulness of loss,
you may find contentment with going on,
finding peace in everyday living.

81. Nourishment

Words can provide nourishment;
nourishment may not be words.
Those who are wise do not always talk;
Those who talk are not necessarily wise.

Can you let go of possessions,
do for others
and find some happiness?
The more you give away,
the more you have.

By not forcing, the Tao provides nourishment.
By following, you will find your way.

Bibliography

Albom, M. Tuesdays with Morrie. New York: Doubleday, 1997.

Buscaglia, L. The Fall of Freddie the Leaf: A Story of Life for All Ages. New York: Henry Holt & Co., 1982

Bombeck, E. I Want to Grow Hair, I Want to Grow Up, I Want to go to Boise: Children Surviving Cancer. New York: Harper & Row, 1989.

Bozarth-Campbell, A. Life is Goodby, Life is Hello: Grieving Well Through All Kinds of Loss. Minneapolis, NM: CampCare Publishers, 1982.

Bridges, W. Transitions: Making Sense of Life's Changes. Reading, MA: Addison-Wesley, 1982.

Byock, I. Dying Well: The Prospect for Growth at the End of Life. New York: Riverhead Books,.1997.

Callanan, M. & Kelley, P. Final Gifts. New York: Bantam Books, 1992.

Childs-Gowell, W. Good Grief Rituals: Tools for Healing. Barrytown, NY: Station Hill Press, 1992.

Cogrove, M. Bloomfield, H. & McWilliams. How to Survive the Loss of a Love. New York: Bantam Books, 1997.

Dass, R., & Gorman, P. How Can I Help? New York: Alfred A. Knopf, 1985.

Doka, K. J., & Davidson, J. (Eds.). Living with Grief when Illness is Prolonged. Washington, DC: Hospice Foundation of America, 1997.

Fassler, J. My Grandpa Died Today. New York: Human Sciences, 1993.

Garant, C. The Tao of the Circles. Atlanta: Humanics, 2000.

Grollman, E. Living When a Loved One has Died. Boston: Becon, 1977.

Huang, T. Laoism: The Complete Teachings of Lao Zi. Atlanta: Humanics, 2000.

Irish, D., Lundquist, K., & Nelson, V. Ethnic Variations in Dying, Grief and Death. Birston, PA: Taylor & Francis, 1993.

Jaffe, C., & Ehrlich, C. (1997). All Kinds of Love: Experiencing Hospice. Amityville, NY: Baywood.

Klass, D., et al., (eds.) Continuing Bonds: New Understandings of Grief. Britsol, PA; Taylor & Francis, 1996.

Kushner, H. When Bad Things Happen to Good People. New York: Shochen Books, 1981.

Longaker, C. Facing Death and Finding Hope. New York: Doubleday, 1997.

Miles, M. Annie and the Old One. Boston: Little-Brown, 1971.

Rando, T. Loss and Anticipatory Grief. Lexington, MA: D.C. Heath, 1986.

Schwartz, M. Morrie: In His Own Words. New York: Dell Publishing, 1996.

Wolfeelt, A. Helping Children Cope with Death. Muncies, IN: Accelerated Development, 1983.

About the Author

Pamela Metz lives in Denver, Colorado where she is an associate professor at the University of Denver Graduate School of Social Work. She teaches a class on the chronically and terminally ill and is a former hospice social worker.

Other Taoist Titles

from Pamela Metz and Humanics

The Tao of Learning
ISBN 0-89334-222-X

The Creative Tao
ISBN 0-89334-255-6

The Tao of Women (with Jacqueline Tobin)
ISBN 0-89334-237-8